A String of Beads

By Pauline Holt

Jazzy Lily

A Light-hearted History of
Glass Beadmaking
in the UK

I'll give my jewels for a set of beads

William Shakespeare - Richard II

Forward:

Very few people have the opportunity to be involved and instrumental in the resurgence of an art form. It began in Stourbridge, considered by many to be the true home of glass making, with one of the few English producers and experts in coloured glass - Plowden and Thompson Ltd, who provided the springboard for glass beadmaking in the UK.

My surname, Beadman, is part of the serendipity that surrounds beadmaking. It is a privilege to write this forward to a book about some of the people who have created a whole new world of artistic opportunity and expression. Pauline Holt is one of these people who have contributed on so many different levels to the success of British beadmaking and this book illustrates the journey.

There are many texts on the technical, artistic, historical and scientific aspects of glass beadmaking but very little on the people of today. The buzz, excitement and can do attitude to beadmaking comes across clearly in this book. The worldwide seeking of knowledge, comradeship, education and harnessing of the technological changes in retailing are wonderfully explored. It is the people and individuality that makes for the fun and excitement - the makers, buyers, collectors and wearers of beads. The Beads Day at Broadfield House Glass Museum is an event not to be missed, and this is the 10th Anniversary. It is accompanied by a competitive exhibition, a lecture evening and the launch of this book, which is being supported by The Friends of Broadfield House Glass Museum.

Barbara P. Beadman

Chairman of The Friends of Broadfield House Glass Museum.   2014
Former Director of Plowden and Thompson Ltd.

Acknowledgments:

I wanted to write this book as it seemed to me a great pity not to have the recent resurgence in glass beadmaking documented in writing. Past generations have missed an opportunity to do this and the history of beadmaking is consequently littered with great gaps of detail. Let us not forget that glass beads can be traced back to 3500 BC in Mesopotamia. Archaeological evidence suggests that the first glass was made in coastal north Syria, (then part of Mesopotamia), and unlike other art forms, glass beads do not disintegrate over time.

This book takes a light-hearted look at relatively recent events, but does not attempt to take account of everything that has happened in the world of beadmaking since the start of the 1970's. It is not a 'History' book.

I have to thank lots of people who have helped me with research and assisted in dating many of the numerous events detailed in the following pages. I would like especially to thank my husband Brian, for all his help and support. Also, Carole Morris and Stefany Tomlin from 'The Bead Society of Great Britain' for supplying some of the old photographs and beads.

Kari Moody and her staff at Broadfield House Glass Museum, for hosting the anniversary exhibition and for her efforts over the past 10 years in helping to organise the annual Beads Day at the Museum.

The Friends of Broadfield House Glass Museum who, with their very generous financial help, made the publication of this book possible. And of course, all the many other people who have helped with details and jolted my memory.

Last, but by no means least, Barbara Beadman, who over the last 17 years has provided me with opportunities that otherwise would never have come my way. At times her enthusiasm and energy seemed never ending! Barbara is well known in virtually every glass related society and organisation in the UK, and even though she has now retired from business, she remains extremely busy, giving her all to every group she is involved with. She continues to provide me with opportunities to demonstrate my skills and she has provided me with so much information for this book. A true friend, thank you Barbara.

Pauline Holt

About the Author
Pauline Holt – Jazzy Lily

Photo by: Des Carrington

My home is in Aylesbury, Buckinghamshire, and the name *'Jazzy Lily'* was thought up by one of my daughters to describe someone who wears bright or outrageous clothes.   So, now that I make bright and colourful jewellery, 'Pauline Holt Jewellery' didn't sound very exciting and so I became *'Jazzy Lily Jewellery'*!

Many moons ago, when I was just 18, I worked for an independent but well-known jeweller in the centre of Manchester - and I loved it.   I enjoyed every aspect of it. Dressing the windows and trying to analyse how much more could be sold using eye catching displays.   In fact, it was the most enjoyable job I have ever had.   So much so, that I decided to attend evening classes in order to learn all about gemmology and eventually I passed my diploma and become a member of the National Association of Goldsmiths.

I have always been passionate about colour, and the prospect of creating something of my own in such a wonderfully tactile material as glass, with a range of such vibrant colours, proved quite challenging but very invigorating.

In 1998 I bought a shed in which to work.   I have said that I am passionate about colour, but let's face it, most garden sheds can be boring, not the sort of working space *'Jazzy Lily'* was going to be happy in! So, I decorated the shed to look like a Caribbean beach hut - inside and out, complete with an imitation thatched roof.   My husband who is used to my crazy ideas was a bit horrified when I asked him to help me thatch the roof.

Mind you, it still becomes something of a talking point and everyone who visits the house has to see the shed. I now have a much larger studio, (shed), minus the thatched roof, where I can accommodate two students keen to learn about making their own glass beads.

My current and larger studio still has a Caribbean look and has been featured in many magazines and newspapers as well as making appearances on the TV programmes, 'The One show' and 'ShedHeads', as well as several other promotional videos.

My New Shed

Although I retired from my job as a finance manager some 5 years ago in order to spend more time making beads and jewellery, I have also enjoyed the time spent teaching beginners in the basic skills of glass beadmaking.

I am always thrilled to see the work they produce following their initial exposure to what is a most wonderful medium.

Over the years I have tried my hand at many crafts and art forms, but I have now found my ultimate passion – making glass beads.

A Light-Hearted History of Beadmaking
1970's to 2014

I should start by stating that I am not an expert when it comes to the history of glass beadmaking. Indeed until I started the research, I had no idea that it would be such a huge task.   Believe me – I could have spent the rest of my life researching this subject.   .

One of the most frustrating facts I have uncovered, is that when some of the ancient societies died out, their methods of making glass beads were buried with them.   Only to be reinvented again and again by later generations.

So, perhaps it will be sensible to begin with the most famous resurgence in glass making, which began in and around Venice several hundred years ago.   In 1292 the glass factories were relocated on to the island of Murano in order to reduce the risk of fire in the city and also to protect the secrets of glass creation.

Secrecy was very important to the Venetians and around four hundred and ninety glass makers were under penalty of death for either revealing their secrets, or for starting up businesses off the island. Because these glassworkers were concentrated into a relatively small area, the re-invention of earlier methods of beadmaking, that had been lost in time, began to re-emerge.   Amongst these practices was the faster and more economical method of manufacture known as the, 'hollow cane drawn method'.

With the exploration of the New World around this time, there came a demand for more beads.   Beads became a sort of currency and were used to purchase slaves, furs and other items.   And so it was that the average European business person travelling abroad could easily achieve a 1000% return on their original investment!

In 1500, there were twenty four glass factories in Murano and by 1606 there were two hundred and fifty bead producers alone.   This dramatic increase in the numbers of beadmakers is due in part to a major cottage industry of wound glass beads.   This manufacturing process became known as 'Lampwork' or 'Flamework' - and these are the terms we still use today.

When I visited Murano in 2003 I could not find a single beadmaking studio, I did however spend £70 on one bead from a small gallery. The owner of the gallery told me that it was made by Mario Zanetti. When I proudly showed it to another beadmaker, I was told that it was not made by Mario but another artist who didn't even work or live on Murano. It is a lovely bead and so I was not too upset, but some homework beforehand may have been of benefit!

Having already admitted that I am no expert with regard to the historical aspects of glass beadmaking, perhaps it would be best if I take a huge leap forward to modern day beadmaking and concentrate primarily on the UK.

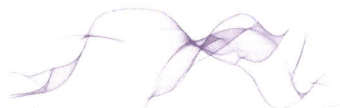

Our Story Starts in the 1970's

Henry Spooner

Henry Spooner, (1905-1996), is a name I hear mentioned whenever someone talks about glass beadmaking in the UK during recent times, but sadly there is precious little written about him or this period. Henry Spooner's wife, Frances became interested in lace making when Barnet College started a bobbin lace making class around 1972. The correct beads for spangling* the bobbins were in short supply. Henry had worked with glass when he trained as an optician and so he began to experiment with old wine and gin bottles and built a kiln in his garage! *(Spangle, a wire loop of glass beads or other ornaments, passing through a hole drilled near the base of a bobbin used in lace-making).

However, the glass he used was not suitable, was full of air bubbles and kept cracking. After some investigation he found a company called Plowden & Thompson Limited (P&T), in Stourbridge. They made coloured glass rods suitable for making beads, so he then set about building his own torch. Initially, his decorative style was perhaps more restricted to coloured swirls and 'blobs'. He did use copper wires for mandrels and he used to etch the wire out with acid, which I should hasten to add, took a couple of days!

He made square cut beads to start with and the lace workers were eager to buy from him. He later progressed to making larger round beads suitable for necklaces. He also started demonstrating his beadmaking skills to various lace groups, and running beadmaking classes.

3

When he eventually gave up beadmaking in the 1990's, due to ill health and failing eyesight, he asked P&T if they knew of anyone who would like to take all of his supplies. They put him in touch with Amanda Glanville and she bought the lot for £25 – but only because he would not accept any more. She thought she might damage the axle of her car on the drive home, so great was the weight of glass she had bought. She is still using some of his glass to this day!

This is a letter he wrote to Amanda on the 28th July 1995

Dear Amanda Glanville

Many thanks for your interesting letter. Advancing years and failing sight caused me to retire five years ago and I disposed of stock and materials.

I got into beadmaking quite by accident, as my wife was teaching lace making and found that glass beads were practically unobtainable by her students [1970]

I discovered that you could melt soda lime glass using two calor gas burners arranged in a V shape (here he drew a diagram). If you wish to use Pyrex glass you will need oxygen as well as calor gas. Plowden & Thompson Glass Works, Stewkins, Stourbridge make the coloured glass rods that are the raw material.

When I was in business I used to run a one day course for potential beadmakers, lunch and all materials for a £5 fee. I still hear from some of my old American and Australian students.
Wishing you all success in your venture.

Sincerely
Henry Spooner.

Although he said he disposed of all his materials, following his death, some two hundred and eighty rods of P&T glass were discovered in his loft - including some colours that the staff and management of P&T had never seen before.

Although I have not managed to find anyone who actually attended one of his classes, Carole Morris of The Bead Society of Great Britain sent me this photograph of some of his beads.

Around the same time that Henry Spooner retired, Douglas Ledger, a competent glass craftsman with controlled skill and a steady hand, used soda glass rods from P&T. He made fairly simple lampwork glass beads around a plain copper wire which was removed later after annealing simply by pulling and stretching the wire! He did not have a great deal of confidence when it came to bead design, but his simple beads went down well with new lace-makers who needed them for their bobbins, (a very trendy revived craft at that time).

Douglas Ledger

Whilst continuing my research and contacting people for information, Doug told me that, "at that time there was absolutely no information about beadmaking and what beadmakers that were around, they all proved to be incredibly secretive".

Doug researched at the British Library and the only information he could find was based on supposition regarding ancient Egyptian beadmakers. Research today has been made so much simpler with the help of the internet!

Moving on Now to the 1990's

In 1993, an article appeared in *Country Living Magazine*, describing Heather Bellman's trip to the USA. On this trip, Heather stayed with an old family friend, beadmaker Kate Drew-Wilkinson.

Heather came back with a suitcase full of glass rods and equipment.   She decided to give up her job and start making her own beads.   Heather then sold her glass jewellery to Liberty's - one of the only artists to have this kind of jewellery in what is regarded as a very prestigious shop.

I remember reading the article very well indeed and thinking to myself, 'wow, I wish I could do that!'

Also in 1993, Diana East (aka Di) got hold of a copy of the USA Society of Glass Beadmakers catalogue and became fascinated by glass beads and how they were made.   She travelled the country in her quest to learn more, looking at Saxon beads in the Yorvik centre and researching how Arabic beads were once made.

During 1994 Diana bought some glass rods from P&T but she had no idea how to make the hole through the centre of the bead.   Until that is, she met Winston Doull.

Winston came to Europe from Zimbabwe, (then known as Rhodesia,) via Asia.   He was living on a Kibbutz in Jerusalem from the 1970's through to the 1990's.   Here he worked with stained glass and experimented fusing glass in a very basic oven.   In the 90's he was invited to study glass blowing at the Bezalel Art Academy in Jerusalem.   It was during this time that he visited Murano and observed the hot glass workers.   What he learned from them lead him to experiment and to start making his own glass beads.

Again he found it almost impossible to buy beadmaking equipment anywhere in Europe.   Even in Murano all the equipment was still homemade and definitely not for sale – they were still very secretive about their processes, but I shouldn't think anyone would have been put to death as they might have been in the 17th century!

Winston Doull

Beads by Winston Doull

During November of 1995, Winston ran a beadmaking course in Lancashire. He set up a simple gas burner for his class using Propylene, (similar to Mapp Gas). This had a big advantage over propane as the glass kept its colour and remained clean. The disadvantage being that it was expensive and difficult to get hold of.

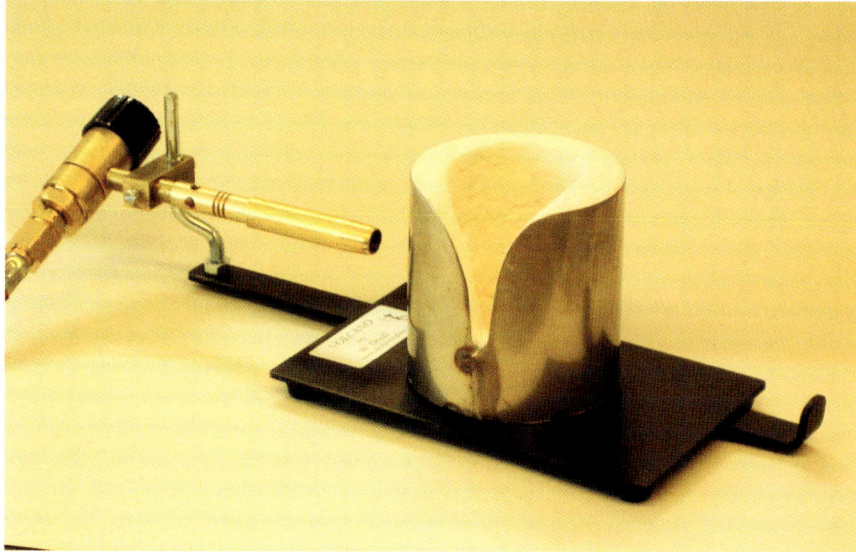

He was also invited to run a couple of courses for Ray Napier in her Studio in Wiltshire and I know three people who did attend this course. They were Ray Napier, Amanda Glanville and Diana East.

Witnessing the use of a mandrel and bead release in order to achieve the hole through the centre of the bead came as a revelation to Di East during Winston's class.

In 1997 Winston finally developed the 'Volcano' torch. It was small, lightweight and used propane and it had the added advantage of flame adjustment. The running costs were cheap and propane was and still is, readily available.

The 'Volcano' is still going strong and is very popular all over Europe, but not so much in the UK. Most beadmakers in the UK use a torch that burns a mixture of propane and oxygen. (Winston now lives in Haan, Germany and still teaches today).

By this time glass beadmaking in the States had taken off in a big way. In 1996 Barbara Beadman, a director of P&T, was a delegate at the Glass Art Society conference in Boston, Massachusetts and this was the first time she had seen beadmaking demonstrations. It was whilst she was chatting to the American beadmaker Stevi Belle that she decided that, "it was about time beadmaking got going in the United Kingdom".

The following year, Barbara - fired with enthusiasm - went to the Glass Art Society conference in Tucson, Arizona and made an agreement with Arrow Springs for them to supply the equipment needed in order to set up classes in the UK. They in turn put her in touch with beadmaking tutor Kate Drew-Wilkinson. Kate was born in England and was, at that time, planning to come back to the UK to visit family and friends.

When Barbara got home, laden with all the tools and torches supplied by Arrow Springs, P&T set up a small room in their glass works in Stourbridge as a classroom. Here they could accommodate around three students and a teacher.

Kate Drew-Wilkinson taught her first class at P&T in the May of 1997. Her students were Lynn Burr, Amanda Glanville and Rennie Bramah.

Di East had a chance conversation with Ray Napier at The Bead Society AGM that year and discovered that they were both keen to find out more about glass beadmaking. Although Di and Ray had both been on the course led by Winston Doull in Lancashire, neither of them had really got to grips with using Winston's, then very basic torch.

Kate Drew-Wilkinson

Sometime later Di bought a Nortel Minor burner from P&T. This torch had been developed by a Canadian, Peter Norton in the 1950's and this solid workhorse torch made a home lampwork studio an affordable possibility. Reliable and virtually indestructible, this torch is still used today by the majority of lampworkers and teaching studios.

Ray then discovered that the person who had taught Heather Bellman was coming to the UK and this was of course, Kate Drew Wilkinson.

Di East enrolled on the next class and Kate was so impressed by her abilities that she invited Di and her daughter to stay with her in Bisbee, Arizona.   The objective being to teach Di more about technique and how to pass these methods on to students so that she could become the resident tutor at P&T.

What a fantastic opportunity that turned out to be.

Bead By Kate Drew Wilkinson

During 1998 and 1999, Di went back to college to study glass at the International Glass Centre in Brierley Hill, West Midlands. That year Rennie Bramah had set up a torch in what had been the college's coal store and yes, Di says that it was as bad as it sounds - the coal store that is!

Also in 1998, Di needed somewhere to work and so her husband Dave converted a room at her home in Enderby, Leicester. Her first student was the late Beverley Edwards.

She now has a purpose built studio and tutors are invited from all over the world to host well attended classes.

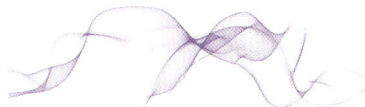

I first met Barbara Beadman at the annual Bead Society of Great Britain Fair in October 1997. She was promoting a beadmaking course at P&T tutored by Diana East. The beautiful selection of glass she had on display fired my enthusiasm no end.

So, in December I made sure that I was one of the delegates. There was no turning back. Before the course had ended I bought all the equipment I needed. When I got home and told my husband that I wanted to erect a shed in our very small garden he was surprised to say the least!

My first shed with thatched roof

My first shed featured in a programme on the TV called *ShedHeads.* After that I had a new larger shed built. John Sergeant, the journalist and TV presenter came to interview me for the BBC1 programme '*The One Show'.* My shed(s) seem to attract more media attention than my beads, unfortunately!

Each year in August, Plowden & Thompson's glass works closed down for two weeks. In the August of 1998, a large area in the works was cleared and a temporary purpose built beadmaking studio was erected. P&T organised an event entitled *'Bring Your Own Burner'*, when beadmakers could bring along their own torch, (if they wished), for a week-long celebration of glass. The event was supported by Business Link and televised on Midlands Today.

Beadmaking class at Bring Your Own Burner 1998

Richard and Barbara Beadman put a tremendous amount of effort into organising this week, Kate Drew-Wilkinson was invited to be our beadmaking expert and we also had visits to several local glass works and studios. On these visits we were offered hands-on experience in a variety of glass art techniques. This was indeed a great event and I am sure that all those delegates who attended this week, now look back on it as a pivotal moment in their education and experiences with glass.

During the *'Bring Your Own Burner'* week several of the delegates and Tutors sat down to discuss the future of beadmaking and how it might be made more inclusive and less secretive. I was one of them and fired with enthusiasm this small group set about putting together some aims, objectives, rules and a constitution - with the plan to meet again soon and form some sort of organisation.

The following year, in the summer of 1999, seven of us got together one very hot Sunday afternoon. We finalised the ideas that had been discussed previously and made the decision to establish Glass Beadmakers UK, (GBUK).

Primarily, we started GBUK because we found it a struggle obtaining information about beadmaking. Courses were few and far between to say the least, and trying to buy equipment was not easy. In fact, the whole thing was enough to put-off the faint-hearted. In those early days, a person had to be totally obsessed with beadmaking in order to carry on. Establishing GBUK would prove a focal point for experienced beadmakers and beginners alike.

Left to right: Diana East, Lyn Burr, Barbara Beadman, Elise Mann, Ray Napier, Pauline Holt. Front: Barbara Mason

We wanted to make this art form far more accessible to everyone. Glass beadmaking **is** an art form, not a craft. However it did take us some time to agree a name, logo and constitution.

From our modest beginnings and the seven founder members, membership grew to twenty nine within a month and within a year it had reached sixty. It never crossed our minds that there might be sixty other people in the country interested in making glass beads!

There were many advantages in being a member of GBUK. Firstly, a quarterly magazine was produced and circulated entitled '*Hot Stuff*'. This was full of interesting articles including tutorials, and other events including members' reports on visits to other countries and courses they had attended. During the research for this book I found back copies of the magazine to be an invaluable tool.

'*Hot Stuff*' is no longer produced and this is a great pity as there will no longer be any documented records of stories and events in the world of UK beadmaking.

GBUK offered a shared tables scheme at various Craft and Bead Fairs. Here GBUK paid for a space at an event and then invited beadmakers to take part - sharing the cost of the space. These events were normally attended by a member of the committee, sales were recorded and the Treasurer then paid the relevant artist their percentage of the overall take. These shared events were very successful and a great help to new beadmakers who did not own display equipment, or for beadmakers who, because of distance could not travel to the event.

Later GBUK arranged a service for members to accept payments via debit/credit cards – thus offering members a cheap and hassle free option which ensured that impulse sales were not lost because a customer did not want to part with cash!

GBUK attended one of these shared events at the Contemporary Glass Society conference at the Eden Project in Cornwall. Yet another example of glass beads being taken seriously by the world of glass.

Committee member, Barbara Mason organised regional meetings when a member could host a meeting at their studio or home. Other beadmakers were invited to attend and they could then swap techniques, show off new tools or just enjoy the company of like-minded people. Each person was encouraged to bring along a plate of food to share, so the host did not have to spend hours cooking at their own expense.

I then set about building a web site for the benefit of members. Each member could have a page of their own and I downloaded their photos, contact details and a brief insight into their work. Of course, this was long before it became commonplace for artists to have their very own web site.

These early days were very exciting and a great opportunity to meet other people who were also hungry for information and inspiration. It was a very friendly group and everyone was happy to share their work and experiences.

Due to this phenomenal increase in glass beadmaking, P&T decided to move their small studio to a much larger space.   This move allowed for eight to ten students at a time to take part in various courses run throughout the year.

In 2000 Barbara Beadman asked me to teach at P&T and also to host a class for the British Scientific Glass Blowers Conference.

The delegates arrived in a minibus in groups of about eight.   Each session lasted for about an hour until the next group arrived.   I lost count of the times the minibus stopped; we didn't have time for a break for lunch - or even a cup of coffee!

Scientific glass blowers work mainly with clear borosilicate glass and most had never used coloured soft glass before.   I am sure you can imagine just how nervous I was, attempting to teach the 'experts' how to make glass beads.   But it turned out to be a very successful day and they certainly enjoyed learning about different ways of working with glass.

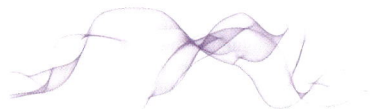

Between 30th July and the 4th August, 2000, P&T arranged a six day *'Glass Extravaganza'*.   Students could come along and discover the many different aspects of working with glass - not just beadmaking.
A similar week to 'Bring your own Burner' in 1998, but this time with different tutors, presentations and glass venues to visit.

Glass Blowing Demo

During March of 2001 Di East and I flew to New York to stay with Barbara Mason who had recently moved to Franklin Lakes, New Jersey.   Our main reason for the visit was to attend several bead fairs in New York City.

When we arrived at LaGuardia Airport, it became apparent that my luggage had been lost in transit and so I was given $200 compensation by the airline company.

We had arranged to be picked up from the airport by Barbara, who was then going to drive us to her house in Franklin Lakes.   Because of the problem with my luggage we were very late coming out through customs. So late in fact, that Barbara thought that we has missed the plane and set off back to Franklin Lakes. When we finally got in touch with her to come back and collect us, it was very late and I seem to remember that we didn't get to bed until about 3 am.

We were rudely awoken at 6 am the following morning when my luggage arrived at Barbara's house. Result! And so between us, we used the $200 for rail fares, lunches and entrance fees to the various bead fairs.   (The weather incidentally was absolutely freezing).

View from Barbara's house in Franklin Lakes.

The beads we saw in the States were amazing. Modern beadmaking was then about ten years ahead of us in the UK and so we were like 'kids in a sweet shop'.   At one of the fairs we met an artist called Nancy Tobey who was teaching later that year in Rochester, New York and she was using coloured borosilicate glass which was something we wanted to try ourselves.

Teal Firstorm Bead by Nancy Tobey

So, in June 2001, Di East and I flew again to New York with the intention of heading for Rochester in 'upstate' New York. Our first night was spent once more with Barbara Mason in Franklin Lakes, New Jersey. (The reason I say 'upstate', is because when we booked the course, we thought that Rochester was in New York City and did not realise that it was a full day's drive 'upstate' to get there. Ah well, that's what you get, for being two small town girls from the UK!)

Planning our route

The course leader was Nancy Tobey and she showed us how to work with coloured borosilicate glass. This glass was difficult to find in the UK and using the coloured variety was a real treat. Now of course, it is widely available and many of us create beads using this type of glass.

Diana Leaving the Liquor Store

Nancy Tobey

On our last night in a little motel on route 104, Di and I decided to run a borosilicate course here in the UK. In 2002 we hired the bead studio at P&T and had a full class for our two day 'BeadZone 104' course – named after route 104! (Must have had something to do with the amount of wine we consumed in the motel that night). Northstar Glass supplied us with enough glass to run the course, completely free of charge.

Because beadmaking as an art form was new and unusual, we used to receive quite a lot of free publicity in those early days. In January 2002 a double page spread appeared in the *Wolverhampton Lifestyle Magazine.*

In December 2001 a photographer was sent along to take some pictures of a course I was leading at P&T just before Christmas. Unfortunately, we picked a bad time of year and consequently we had no students. My husband Brian, Barbara and Richard Beadman had to be roped in to act as 'students' for the day, for the benefit of the camera.

The photographer was contracted to be there for around half-an-hour or so, take some pictures and go. Some three and a half hours later he was still attempting to perfect a small bead of his own that he wanted to make for his three year old daughter. Another budding beadmaker was hooked!

Here we see the photographer lying on his back taking a picture of some glass beads which had been balanced on a sheet of glass and using the sky as a background.

Today we still receive a lot of free publicity. Many beadmakers have appeared on mainstream TV programmes including the BBC1' s '*The One show'* and *Michael Portillo's, 'Great British Railway Journeys'.*

Also, many national newspapers have featured photographs of beadmakers work and their studios and regular articles and tutorials often appear in specialist bead magazines.

During '*Open Studios'* weeks around the country, the number of beadmakers taking part increases each year.

I am sure that this publicity will continue in the future.

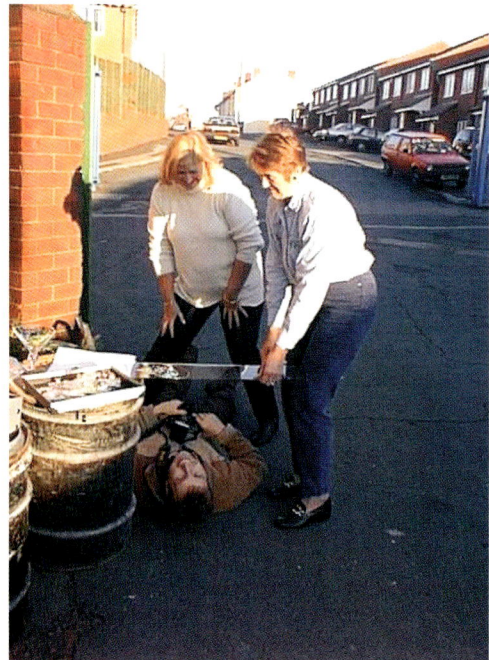

During 2002 Di East, Beverley Edwards and myself attended the International Society of Glass Beadmakers Gathering, (conference), in Alexandria, Virginia.

I entered the silly bead competition with a pair of beads called *Louis and Julie Chihuly*, a satirical take-off of the famous glass artist Dale Chihuly. I did not win, but more of that later.

Aladdin's Palace Bead

During that week in Alexandria, there was a charity bead auction and one of Di's beads, 'Aladdin's Palace', sold for an incredible $625 - the most ever paid for a single bead (at that time), in the United States.

Left to right: Pauline Holt, Beverley Edwards, Diana East

Beverly Edwards, who I mentioned earlier, started in business at the age of 19. She used bought-in beads to make jewellery (as most of us did), until she decided to make her own beads and took a class with Diana East.

She went on to make beautiful borosilicate glass beads mounted into sophisticated gold and silver jewellery.

Her creations were sold under the trade name of Mirage Jewellery at Ruthin Craft Centre. Very sadly, Beverley died of cancer in 2012 aged just forty three.

The photo on the right shows one of her beautiful necklaces.

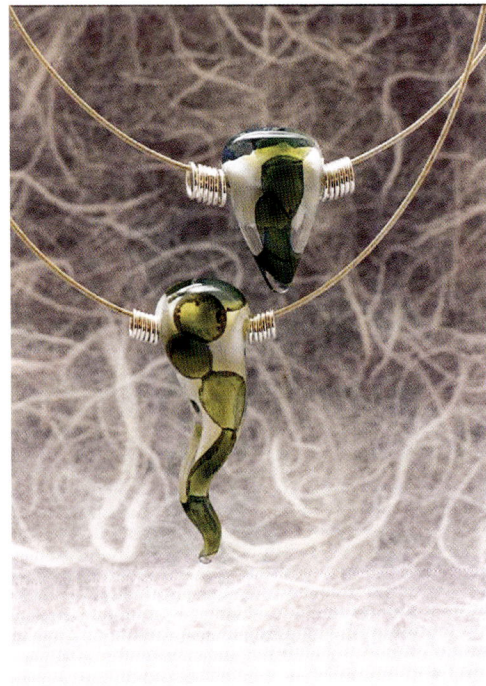

During 2003, I was invited to demonstrate at an Art Exhibition in Portugal. It was claimed by the organisers that glass beadmaking was something that had never been seen in Portugal before. Unlike events in the UK, but just like events in Spain and Portugal, the venue did not open until about 6pm and closed after midnight. I went to bed absolutely shattered. Judging from Google searches made since, we are still waiting for beadmaking to take off in Portugal. Ah well, you can't win 'em all.

Art Exhibition in Portugal

Moving on now to other notable events which indicate just how much beadmaking has been accepted by glass professional bodies.

The Contemporary Glass Arts Society invited Kate Drew-Wilkinson, sponsored by P&T, to give classes at their Conference in the newly opened Sunderland Glass Centre and these classes have continued to bring training and work into this part of the north east.

The Icelandic Consulate, in Norway, considered beadmaking as a form of training for disabled students, asking if I would act as tutor. Unfortunately, after much consideration, the project was shelved.

In 2011 **The Worshipful Company of Glass Sellers** of London asked me to make 250 mobile phone/handbag charms using a glass bead. Pairs of these charms were to be given as gifts to the ladies attending their Annual Banquet at the Mansion House. The then Master, Martin Scarth and his wife came to my studio on a couple of occasions to select the style of beads they wanted, and the commemorative cards and boxes to accompany the beads. It was hard work to produce so many beads, but it was worth it and it seems that the ladies were pleased with their gift.

British Glass - British Glass Manufacturers Confederation is instrumental in promoting glass as first choice material across all glass sectors and ensuring that both the industry and its products remain competitive, innovative and are not unnecessarily or disproportionately hindered by new regulation, standards or legislative changes. They act as the industry's focal point, playing the principal role in communicating the concerns and aspirations of their Members to the Government, the European Union and other external interest groups and trade bodies. So quite a serious organisation and not really part of the Art Glass world.

In 2013 I was asked to demonstrate at their annual conference in Manchester. Again, I was rather nervous about talking to such knowledgeable delegates. I need not have worried, it was a wonderful day, most of the delegates wanted to have-a-go themselves - and I sold quite a lot of glass bead jewellery too! I have been invited to take part again this year (2014) in London.

I am certain that many other glass beadmakers have other stories of their own that could form part of our recent history. It is a missed opportunity, I think, that there is no 'hub' available at the moment where stories, successes and experiences can be stored or enjoyed by other beadmakers.

Glass Beadmakers UK (GBUK)

GBUK was founded in 1999 and over the years its members have included several pioneers from the UK glass beadmaking fraternity.   The society owes its establishment to the resurgence of interest in lampworking in the USA.   A few of these bold American souls, talented beadmakers in their own rite, braved the challenge of awakening lampworking skills in the UK.

They could not have imagined just how successful they were going to be.   First among these was Kate Drew-Wilkinson, who along with the facilities provided by Barbara Beadman at P&T taught many of us the basics of lampworking.   Their enthusiasm, skill and encouragement, together with that of many GBUK members, have been responsible for keeping the 'flame' alive.

The Objectives of GBUK:

- The sharing and dissemination of information on glass beadmaking through networking
- The furtherance of educational opportunities in order to facilitate the art of glass beadmaking

Regular membership is open to all people who have an interest in the methods and processes of making glass beads.

Honorary membership is allocated by committee vote. Current Members:

Kate Drew-Wilkinson, Kate Fowle Meleney, Barbara Beadman, Diana East, Amanda Glanville, Pauline Holt, Barbara Mason, Martin Tuffnell and Richard Downton.

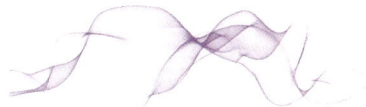

Stourbridge Bead Fair at the Bonded Warehouse

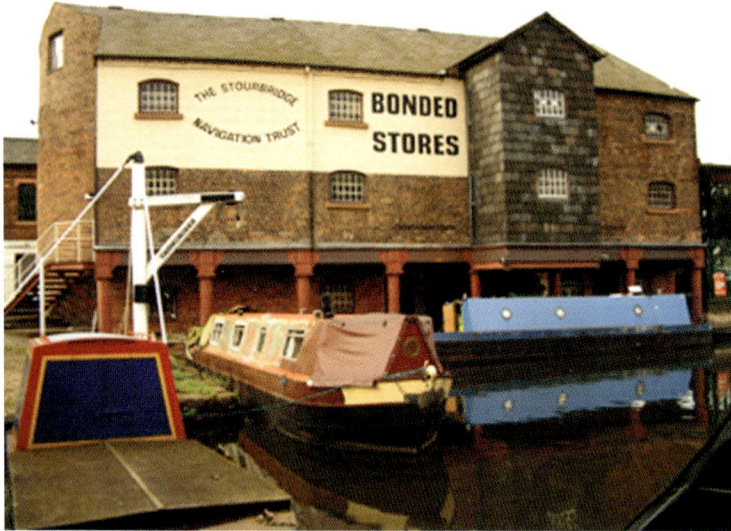

This bead fair began life in 2004 and it was initially staged by Glass Beadmakers UK. It was the first fair to feature mainly handmade glass beads, although there were also other stalls selling beadmaking equipment and jewellery findings. Nevertheless, its priority was to showcase and promote the art of glass beadmaking.

Since 2005 the fair has been organised and managed by Pat and Roy Ayre of Gallowglass and it has become an important event for artists and the local community alike.

Since those early days, the number of beadmakers in this country has increased massively, and handcrafted glass beads are now more common place at specialist bead fairs and exhibitions. The public still remain fascinated as they watch glass rods being turned into glass beads. Although the number of beadmakers has increased, we continue to explore opportunities to promote the art and bring it to new artists, in an effort to grow the medium.

The fair is still held every year at the end of August, during the bank holiday weekend and every two years the event is open for two days when it coincides with the International Festival of Glass.

The International Festival of Glass & British Glass Biennale

The International Festival of Glass (IFG) is the only UK based Festival celebrating the spectacle, drama and excitement of glassmaking.   Attracting visitors from all over the world, the event takes place biennially in the Stourbridge Glass Quarter.

It features a world class exhibition and master classes are held covering a range of techniques.   The festival is staged at several venues around Stourbridge and it succeeds in both inspiring and amazing artists and the general public.

In 2006 I decided to do some more work on my *Louis and Julie Chihuly* beads, made originally in 2004 for the 'Silly Bead' competition in the USA.   I re-invented my design and turned it into a wearable necklace and low and behold, it was chosen as an exhibit for the 2006 International Glass Festival Biennale.   You could say that I was delighted, but that would be an understatement!

That same year a bead made by Diana East was also chosen. One of the first years in which beads were included in the IFG exhibition. Finally, beads had been accepted as a serious form of glass art.

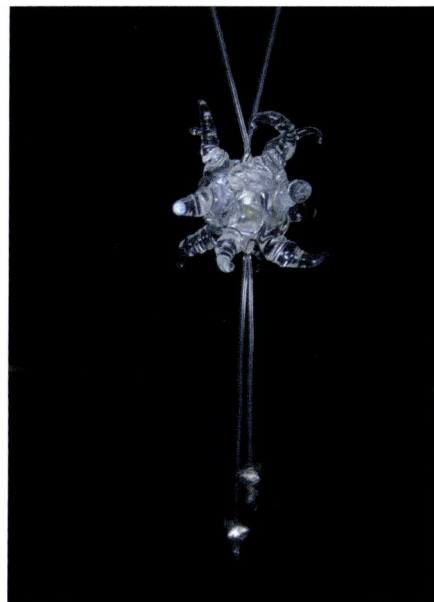

Catwalk necklace (Julie)

In 2010, a third bead artist was also chosen, Rowan van der Holt, (no relation), with her beautiful sculptured flower tiara.

The Tempest Exhibition 2008

This exciting exhibition was conceived by Diana East as a showcase for the miniature art form of glass beads to run in conjunction with the International Festival of Glass 2008

Several internationally renowned glass artists were challenged to try their hands at this tiny scale of work alongside well known and up- and- coming glass bead artists.

A most auspicious star
Pauline Holt

Photo by Lucy Hunt

H 2.8cm, W 3cm, D 1.5cm

Lampworked
using Borosilicate glass with
etched dichroic glass stars

'By accident most strange,
bountiful fortune,
Now my dear lady,
hath mine enemies
Brought to this shore;
and by my prescience
I find my zenith doth depend upon
a most auspicious star,
whose influence
If now I court not but omit,
my fortunes
Will ever after droop.'

Act 1 Scene 2 : Prospero
William Shakespeare

The objective was to present interpretations of Shakespeare's play, *The Tempest* in the form of one sculptural glass bead.   The small scale of these objects belied their complexity and the skill required to produce them.   All of the finished beads were displayed in the exhibition and were seen by hundreds of visitors.

Seventy artists took part, the exhibition then travelled to several UK venues, as well as to the USA, France and Germany.

Rachel Elliott's *'Rhombicosidodecahedron'* bead was created using sixty small pieces of glass. It was then painted using traditional enamels in an effort to replicate the storm in Shakespeare's play.

Photo by Lucy Hunt

This bead is featured on the cover of the book that accompanied the Tempest exhibition.

The UK Flame Off

The 'UK Flame Off' is a three day event run *by* lampwork artists *for* lampwork artists.   Martin Tuffnell of **Tuffnell Glass,** together with Simon Robinson of **Totally Beads,** have been running this event every year since 2008.   It began as a small show bringing glass beadmakers together from all over the UK.

Martin and Simon have been successful in persuading leading lampworkers from around the world to attend this event to teach and demonstrate their own unique styles and techniques to an assembled audience.

Visitors are encouraged to try out new tools and equipment before buying, and to share information and techniques with other artists. Hundreds of glass beadmakers have been brought together since 2008, in order to allow them to 'play' with glass and fire.   (Sounds like a Health and Safety nightmare doesn't it?)

For the first five years, the event was held at Towcester Race Course where the first floor of the main building could accommodate more than one hundred and fifty people in a theatre style layout.

Some of the best lampwork artists in the world have demonstrated in front of the camera - the images being relayed on to large screen TV's.   This makes it easy for the audience to see at close quarters all aspects of the lampworker's art and technique.

Also on site is a sales area, a 'lampworker's village', where leading artists can sell their creations and a huge 'taster' area.   The 'taster' area has tables and benches set out for anyone to sit and experiment with glass, make their own very first bead or pendant or just melt and 'blob'

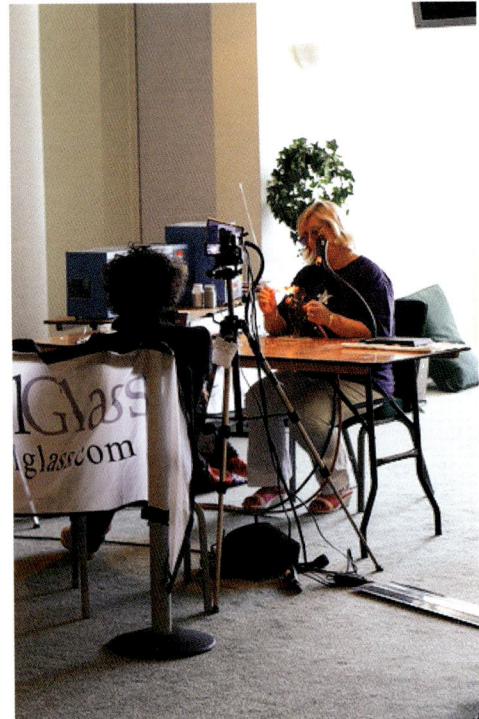

Pauline Holt at the Flame Off 2009

If you have never made beads or 'played' around with hot glass before, but have always wanted to, then this is the show for you.   Help is also available from the on-site stewards and if you have really enjoyed the experience, then you can buy all the required equipment and take it home with you! What could be better?

Tuffnell Glass was founded by Bill Tuffnell.   The first beads he produced were also for lace makers and were small 6mm square beads with a criss-cross pattern on all four sides.   From that first design, Bill soon expanded and began to produce round and oval beads.   For the first three years of operation, Bill's beads were made from off- cuts of stained glass.

Bill's son, Martin, now runs the company and he can be seen demonstrating the art of glass beadmaking at almost all of the bead fairs held in this country.

Tuffnell Glass is now one of the UK's major suppliers of beadmaking tools and they carry an extensive range of glass rods.

Plowden & Thompson Limited

Plowden & Thompson Limited, based at the Dial Glass works in Stourbridge in the heart of the Glass Quarter, played a huge part in the success of glass beadmaking in the UK.

The Dial Glassworks was constructed in 1788 and is the last remaining working cone in Europe; although minus its top which was removed some 80 years ago and was replaced by a remarkable self-supporting roof.

They manufactured their own glass rods in a range of vibrant colours and sold all the equipment required for making glass beads. Whilst beadmaking was only a small part of their business, the directors, Richard and Barbara Beadman, put in a huge amount of time and effort in order to ensure that glass beadmaking became a success in the UK.

They turned part of their factory into a studio capable of accommodating eight to ten students. They recruited experienced glass artists from all over the world to come and mentor courses. And, for two years running, they hosted a week of glass bead courses and visits to other glass studios so that students could obtain a good understanding of the glass industry and art glass.

Tutors from all over the world were invited to host courses, they include:

Kate Drew-Wilkinson – USA
Shane Ferro - USA
Kate Fowle Meleney - USA
Alex & Emily Lake – New Zealand
Lezlie Levitt-Wineberger – Canada
Dora Schubert - Germany
Loren Stump – USA

Shane Ferro Demonstrating

Talented beadmakers from the UK also regularly taught at P&T:

Roy Ayre	Neil Harris
Gillian Blum	Philip Hartley
Rennie Bramah	Pauline Holt
Julia Ann Denton	Barbara Mason
Diana East	Bob Martin
John Harris	Steve Ramsey

During 2013, Richard and Barbara Beadman retired and sold the business. Although they are no longer involved with Plowden & Thompson Limited, they are still very much involved in the glass business. Sadly the new owners no longer make or sell glass rods.

Broadfield House Glass Museum

Broadfield House and its original grounds, situated in Kingswinford, just north of Stourbridge, dates back to the 18th century and was privately owned until 1943.   It was bought by a local industrialist who then began selling off separate portions of the surrounding estate.

From 1978 it remained empty for two years before Dudley Council reopened it as a Museum.
Their vision was to showcase the glass making traditions and heritage of nearby Stourbridge.

In 1994 the Council added an all-glass pavilion to the rear of the existing building providing a new entrance, exhibition space and shop area.   This addition also provides a link through to the glass making studio.   This structure won an award and was then the largest glass structure in Europe (i.e. no metal or wooden supports)

Late in 1993 a group of glass enthusiasts decided to form a Friends organisation for the Museum. The first meeting was held at Dudley Art Gallery in March 1994, and The Friends were delighted and honoured that Mary Boydell, from Sotheby's in Ireland, gave the inaugural lecture.

At present there are more than three hundred members throughout the world and eighteen corporate members.   Members' interests range from those interested in the local history to avid glass collectors and researchers.

The Friends support the work of the Museum through a range of activities.   One, The Friends Purchase Fund, was set up following local government's decision to end the museum's acquisition budget.   This fund allows the museum to make purchases of new acquisitions and money is raised via general fund-raising and match funding for grant applications.   To date, more than £50,000 has been raised in this way by The Friends to help with the ongoing purchase of items new to Broadfield House.

Other activities organised by The Friends, called the Facets programme, includes an annual series of lectures on glass topics by guest speakers, visits to glass factories and studios, talks on major exhibitions at the Museum, providing refreshment facilities at events, and a Christmas party.   These events provide opportunities for fund-raising, learning and, of course, enjoyment.

Each year The Friends of Broadfield House Glass Museum make a monetary award to one or more part time students taking a glass course at Dudley College.   If more than one student is selected, then the award is divided between them.   The lucky recipient is chosen on the grounds of progress made, quality of work and an input from their tutor.

The very first 'Bead Collectors Day' was held in September 2004 at the Museum.   Di East demonstrated in the Studio and Stefany Tomlin identified antique and ancient beads brought in by visitors.   This day was a great success and the "Beads Day" has now become an annual event held in May each year.

Since 2005 I have worked closely with the museum in organising the annual Beads Day. Artists are invited to demonstrate in the studio, specially set up for the day with lampworking equipment and seating for visitors.

Roy Ayre Demonstrating at the museum
Photo by Richard Downton

We also have display and sales tables situated in other rooms in the museum. The event is open to the public and is usually a very busy day - for both the museum, and beadmakers alike. Yet again, visitors are amazed to witness for the first time, a bead being made from a rod of glass.

Photo by Richard Downton

In most of these years, GBUK has displayed work by other members and this was organised by Barbara Mason who, by now had moved back to the UK.   The purpose of GBUK's presence was to attract new members and outline the aims and objectives of the society.

Photo by Richard Downton

Since those early days, the following beadmakers have demonstrated their skills at this event:

2005 Sarah Downton, Amanda Glanville, Pauline Holt
2006 Roy Ayre, Sarah Downton, Amanda Glanville, Judith Johnson
2007 Roy Ayre, Sarah Downton, Pauline Holt
2008, Beverley Edwards, Pauline Holt, Lesley McFarland, Liz Parker
2009 Francesca Cerreta, Beverley Hicklin, Pauline Holt
2010 Pauline Holt, Marlene Minhas, Lorna Prime
2011 Min Fidler, Pauline Holt, Ema Kelly,
2012 Pauline Holt, Marlene Minhas, Heather Pearce, Rachael Warren,
2013 Julie Fountain, Pauline Holt, Lesley Nixon,

Sarah Downton Photo by Richard Downton

Some quotes from Beads Day attendees

"The Bead Day event at Broadfield House Glass Museum in Stourbridge on Saturday was brilliant, I loved it. I didn't have enough time to explore the museum properly, so a visit when I'm not selling my work or demonstrating lampwork is definitely on the cards. I was almost afraid to take on board what I was seeing as I rushed past the display cases of beautiful glass exhibits, they were so impressive. Fabulous" - Min Fidler. May 2011

"The Beads Day is one of the most popular events in the museum's calendar. The displays and demonstrations explore the colourful world of beads, with plenty to interest both experts and beginners" - Councillor Tracy Wood, Dudley Council.

And so, this year (2014), we shall be celebrating the 10th anniversary of the Beads Day.
To mark the occasion several UK beadmakers were asked to submit samples of their work, and twenty nine of these artists were chosen to be included in an exhibition at the Museum.

Photographs of these beautiful beads are included on the following pages, and they show how beadmaking has progressed in this country since the 1970's. This diverse collection of beads was selected from beginners to experienced artists; they show some innovative and unusual ways in which glass beads can be made.

The exhibition will also include some beads from other influential artists which have kindly been donated by bead historians and enthusiasts.

The following pages mark the 10th anniversary of the Beads Day at Broadfield House Glass Museum.
All of the beads shown will be on display from 10th May until September 2014

Julie Anne Denton

Info@JulieAnneDenton.com
www.JulieAnneDenton.com
Isle of Man & Switzerland

PRiMiTiV3

This piece is hand-formed in the flame, using Borosilicate glass and powders.

'Julie Anne Denton'

Sarah Brown – The Tartan Trout

sarah@thetartantrout.co.uk
www.thetartantrout.co.uk
High Bickington, Devon

Rainbow Blossom

This rainbow blossom has been created using Effetre glass for the colours and Double Helix Zephyr for the clear.   I have used a Pegasus round bead roller to help with the shape.

'Sarah Brown'

Madeline Bunyan

mail@madelinebunyan.com
www.madelinebunyan.com
Dawlish, Devon

Flower Owl

Silver glass, with its beautiful shimmering colours has featured in my work for some time, as have sculptural beads, but until recently, they have always been separate. The best bead designs to me are those that have evolved, taken time, elements from other beads, the whole becomes greater than the sum of its parts.

'Madeline Bunyan'

Ingrid Brunt

parsley1@blueyonder.co.uk
www.bruntiesbeads.com
Mansfield, Notts.

Potion Class Disaster Photo by Sarah Midgley
My fun set of beads tells a story. A young witch with her cauldron exploding and potion flying everywhere, onto her crooked hat and unlucky cat. The four focal and eleven spacer beads are made from CIM Hades and Effetre pale green and pea green glass.

'Ingrid Brunt'

Diana East

dianaeast@glass2wear.com
www.glass2wear.com
Enderby, Leicester

Blue Angel
Mandrel wound Effetre glass bead with enamel, silver glass, silver foil and stainless steel armatures with smaller parts attached. Carved and polished. 75 mm high.

'Diana East'

Geraldine Kaminski

g_z_k@hotmail.com
http://www.etsy.com/shop/StrikingLampwork
Dundee

Tortoise

For this bead I've used copper/green Effetre glass to form the body of the tortoise and silvered ivory for the pattern on the shell with dark brown for the body.

'Geraldine Kaminski'

Ilsa Fatt

ilsa@glass-mountain.co.uk
www.glass-mountain.co.uk
Bristol

Fire Dancing

Long necklace of lampworked beads in red, orange, yellow and black, interspersed with sections of woven beadwork in the same colour scheme. 104 glass with twisties and raised dot trails, pressed with an Ellipse Crunch press and featuring a ruffle on one side. Also spacer beads featuring small dots and twisties.

'Ilsa Fatt'

Julie Fountain, Lush Lampwork

Julie@lushlampwork.com
www.lushlampwork.com
Malvern, Worcs.

Seashore Necklace
All of the beach themed beads are made from Italian soft glass. The three pressed lentil focals are decorated with fine silver and my own handmade murrini. Two smaller pressed lentils are textured to resemble shells and the closure is a shank button with a rock-pool design. The spacer beads are made from a two tone glass.

'Julie Fountain'

Helen Gorick – Helen G Beads

hgorick@yahoo.co.uk
www.helengbeads.co.uk
Honiton, Devon

Petal Reflections

Multiple layers of opaque, bright transparent colours and clear have been added in various ways to produce a bead with lots of depth and interest. The centre has been overlaid with alternate wraps of opaque and transparent colours, and then carefully manipulated with tools to produce a design to complement the petal effect within the bead.

'Helen Gorick'

Manda Muddimer – Mangobeads

info@mangobeads.co.uk
www.mangobeads.co.uk
Barnstaple, Devon

Harlequin Pendant

Lampwork glass bead soft glass COE 104 Effetre, CIM, Lausha, Double Helix. The design is my own and based on my Harlequin Cab Tutorial. The pendant back is handmade by us in sterling silver and set into the back of the cabochon.

'Manda Muddimer'

Sarah Jones

Sarahjones@theglassshed.co.uk
www.theglassshed.co.uk
Stourbridge.W. Midlands

Candlestick

I have made a beaded candlestick using bicycle sprockets.
The beads have been made using a variety of techniques,
using Effetre soda lime glass rods dimensions: height 230mm
width of base 115mm.

'Sarah Jones'

Judith Johnston

judith@judith-johnston.com
www.judith-johnston.com
Hove, East Sussex

Florescence

Purple floral bicone bead. Decorated with flowers with cubic zirconia
centres, pink flower murrini and butterfly murrini, (butterfly made by
Ryan Turner).

'Judith Johnston'

48

Pauline Holt - Jazzy Lily

pauline@jazzylily.com
www.jazzylily.com
Aylesbury, Bucks.

Buttercups & Daisies

Yellow is not a colour used very often but I thought this would make an attractive necklace. These simple beads are made from a mixture of different glass - Bullseye, Plowden & Thompson, and Reichenbach. The beads have been incorporated onto a macramé cord with a silver clasp.

'Pauline Holt'

Lesley Silver – Beadsashore

Beadsashore@yahoo.co.uk
or mail@beadsashore.com
www.Beadsashore.com
St Ives, Cornwall

Fireworks Photo: Stewart Girvan
Discs of mixed colours of Italian Effetre glass woven into a two layer collar style necklace.

'Lesley Silver'

Phoebe Joy

pj@phoebejoy.co.uk
www.phoebejoy.co.uk
Loughborough, Leics.

Icing on the Cake

A handcrafted necklace made with individual lampworked beads. I have used soft pastel Effetre glass colours in multiple combinations, to create an asymmetric look. I use a technique of carefully dotting balls of glass on top of each other; this creates delicate patterns reminiscent of icing on a cake.

'Phoebe Joy'

Catherine Arrowsmith

catherine.neil80@gmail.com
www.arrowsmithglassart.com
Wellingborough, Northants.

Polychromatic Serpent Photo by Stuart Thomson

The glass used to make the polychromatic serpent is a mixture of Effetre and Reichenbach glass.
 The head was made on a blow pipe so as to make it lighter in weight, the colours were chosen for their boldness and vigour. In the middle there is a copper wire to give the piece structure and strength.

'Catherine Arrowsmith'

Barbara Mason

bjm@glass-beads.co.uk
www.glass-beads.co.uk
Swindon, Wiltshire

Alhambra

Inspired by a visit to the Alhambra Palace in Granada. Lampworked soda-lime glass, heat, marver and gravity shaped, stringer decoration, raked, 38mm x 17mm.

'Barbara Mason'

John Mason ✗ Ingridpears husband

j.mason.72@hotmail.com
www.ingridpears.com
Mansfield, Notts.

Best of Friends

Soda glass, hand-formed, Effetre rods and stringers.

'John Mason'

Gay Massender – GaysieMay

gaysiemay@live.co.uk
www.gaysiemay.etsy.com
Scarborough, N. Yorks

Grey Area

This piece is a brooch and does include a string of beads. However, I wanted to show the diversity of lampwork glass and so have used glass headpins, simply shaped with a marver and an old kitchen knife. The headpins are then woven together to form the brooch and the string of beads hangs below.

'Gay Massender'

Marlene Minhas – Glassygear

glassygear@yahoo.com
Edgware, Middx.

Red Baroque   Photo by Pauline Holt

Simple rods of glass can be manipulated in many ways. "Baroque" means extravagantly ornate. This bead uses a combination of different glass types, has been hand shaped, and uses a reduction flame to bring out the shine of the silver rich glass. A bit of bling is born.

'Marlene Minhas'

Suzie Sullivan

suzie@derryauncrafts.com
www.derryauncrafts.com
Westport, Co. Mayo

Briar & Rose

This bracelet and ring is inspired by the song 'The Briar and the Rose'. The bracelet is constructed by embellishing lengths of copper wire with flame worked glass flowers. Starting with two 'spokes' the rubber weaver is intertwined, as the weaving progresses more wire spokes are added and 'cast off' to create the desired shape.

'Suzie Sullivan'

Keren Panthaki

vasdea@me.com
www.vasdea.wordpress.com
Horsell, Surrey

Watercolour Tulips *Photo: Trevor Aston*
Focal bead: (40 mm) soda lime glass, frit, hand pulled stringer, pressed and etched. Sculptural bead and accent lampwork beads: soda lime glass, hand pulled stringer, etched.
Necklace: lampwork focal and sculptural bead, turquoise faceted agate, lampwork accents beads, handmade sterling silver clasp and pendant holder.

'Keren Panthaki'

Carol Hennahane

carol.hennahane@btinternet.com
Marks Tey, Essex

Seaweed
My work is derived from the study of fragile environmental boundaries and the sustainability of life. I have used Effetre glass, silver stringer, silver wire and dual colour encasing. Bronze wire, which will gain a patina over time, has been manipulated and hammered to form a necklace which fastens with handmade clasp at the front.

'Carol Hennahane'

Mandy Southan

enquiries@mandysouthan.co.uk
www.mandysouthan.co.uk
Hastings, East Sussex

Silver Leopard Beads

Lampworked, ivory and silver glass leopard spot beads with a central focal, striped and spiralled into tiny green 'cat's eyes'. Made with Murano and silver reduction glass, the lentil-shaped beads range from 1.8cm to 2.6cm (3/4" to 1") diameter and the necklace is completed with sterling silver.

'Mandy Southan'

Claire Morris – Rowanberry Designs

rowanberryglass@gmail.com
www.rowanberrydesigns.co.uk
Newcastle, Staffs.

Snowdonia Mountain Tree

A lampwork glass bead featuring a mountain landscape inspired by Snowdonia with a raised mountain ash tree in berry on the front. Is made of soft glass and a vast array of specially designed hand pulled stringers and canes to "paint" the design on. It has been acid etched for a frosted matt feel.

'Claire Morris'

Becky Haywood – Chameleon Designs

becky@chameleondesigns.co.uk
www.chameleondesigns.co.uk
Wem, Shrops.

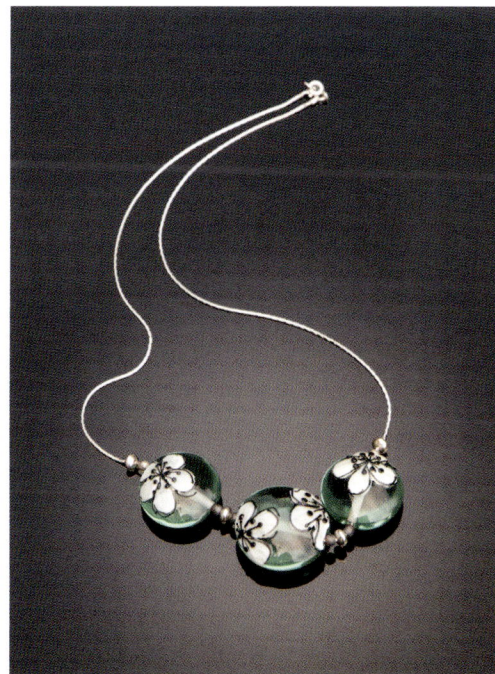

Illustrated Beads

Large soft glass lentils decorated with blossom "illustrations" inspired by my own drawings, which have been 'drawn' on to the bead with stringers (thin rods of glass).

'Becky Haywood'

Charlotte Verity

info@charlotteverity.com
www.charlotteverity.com
Salford, Lancs.

Purple Bubble Chain Necklace
Hollow, blown-glass 'bubbles' in varying shades of purple; some are all one shade, while others have multi-tonal swirling or mottled patterns. A few are sandblasted, while occasional bubbles are blown from colourless glass and filled with tiny faceted stones. All the bubbles are annealed for durability and fixed to a handmade sterling silver multi-link chain.

'Charlotte Verity'

Sue Webb

sue.bramallwebb@virginmedia.com
www.suewebb.co.uk
Bristol

Turtle beach
This bead is typical of the animal inspired beads I like to make, some of which are beads and others are ornamental.

'Sue Webb'

Amy Whittingham

amywhittingham@yahoo.co.uk
Glassbyamy.co.uk
Plymouth, Devon

Mohawk skull Photo: Lloyd Russell
Inspired by the Day of the Dead and the Mexican sugar skulls and steampunk jewellery. I have created this unique cast glass skull, individually hand carved, using a combination of lampworked glass horns and lost wax casting. The glass combines to make this stunning pendant, intricate in its detail and delicate, with a frosted finish.

'Amy Whittingham'

Bead artists who teach Glass Beadmaking listed by area

Town/County	Name (Nos. yrs experience)	Contact Details
Aylesbury, Bucks	Pauline Holt - Jazzy Lily (16 yrs)	pauline@jazzylily.com www.jazzylily.com
Barnstaple, Devon	Manda Muddimer - Mangobeads (8 yrs)	info@mangobeads.co.uk www.mangobeads.co.uk
Bristol	Sue Webb (8 yrs)	suebramallwebb@virginmeadia.com www.suewebb.co.uk
Dawlish, Devon	Madeline Bunyan (7yrs)	mail@madelinebunyan.com www.madelinebunyan.com
Enderby, Leicester	Diana East (20yrs)	dianaeast@glass2wear.com www.glass2wear.com
Honiton, Devon	Helen Gorick – Helen G Beads (6yrs)	hgorick@yahoo.co.uk www.helengbeads.co.uk
Horsell, Surry	Keren Panthaki (8yrs)	vasdea@me.com www.vasdea.wordpress.com
Isle of Man & Switzerland.	Julie Anne Denton (17yrs)	Info@JulieAnneDenton.com www. JulieAnneDenton.com
Malvern, Worcs	Julie Fountain, Lush Lampwork (6yrs)	Julie@lushlampwork.com www.lushlampwork.com
Mansfield, Notts	John Mason (3yrs)	j.mason.72@hotmail.com www.ingridpears.com
Marks Tey, Essex	Carol Hennahane (3yrs)	carol.hennahane@btinternet.com
Plymouth, Devon	Amy Whittingham (3yrs)	amywhittingham@yahoo.co.uk www.Glassbyamy.co.uk

Scarborough, N. Yorks.	Gay Massender - GaysieMay (6yrs)	gaysiemay@live.co.uk
		www.gaysiemay.etsy.com
St Ives, Cornwall	Lesley Silver - Beadsashore (6 yrs)	Beadsashore@yahoo.co.uk
		www.Beadsashore.com
Stourbridge. W. Midlands	Sarah Jones (5yrs)	Sarahjones@theglassshed.co.uk
		www.theglassshed.co.uk
Swindon, Wiltshire	Barbara Mason (16 yrs)	bjm@glass-beads.co.uk
		www.glass-beads.co.uk
Wem, Shrops	Becky Haywood - Chameleon Designs (7 yrs)	becky@chameleondesigns.co.uk
		www.chameleondesigns.co.uk

Basic Equipment Needed for Making Glass Beads

Selection of Glass Rods

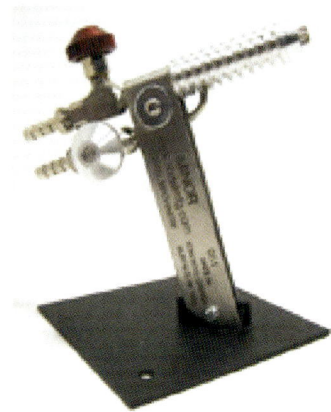

Nortel Minor Burner

Didymium Glasses

Annealing Kiln

Small tools:
Bead Release and Mandrels, Graphite Paddles & Shapers/Presses, Tweezers, Glass Rod Cutters, Rod Rest. For beginners, less expensive equipment is available.

How to Make a Basic Hot Glass Bead

1. Using a lampworker's torch, gently heat a rod of glass until molten.

2. Gently touch the mandrel with the hot glass and wind the hot glass around the mandrel.

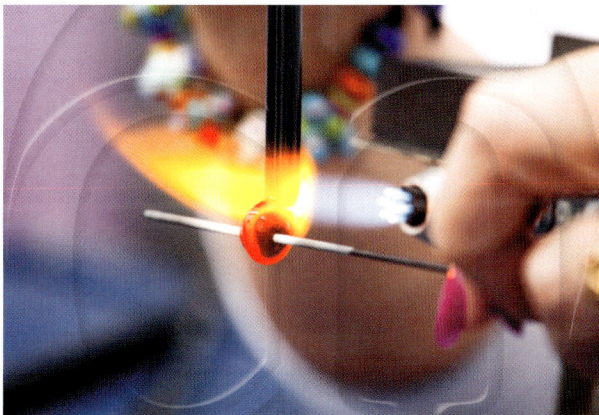

3. To make a larger bead add more glass and shape by rotating the mandrel, and with the help of gravity & surface tension make a round bead.

4. Allow the bead to cool slightly. Apply decoration with another coloured rod or glass stringer (a very thin rod of glass). Place the hot bead in an annealing kiln and allow cooling down for at least 12 hours.

These are very basic steps to making a glass bead, and have been photographed through a safety screen.
To learn more, contact one of the artists listed.

Useful Web Sites

Glass and beadmaking tools and equipment:

www.tuffnellglass.co.uk
www.creativeglassshop.co.uk
off-mandrel.com
www.glassstudiosupplies.co.uk

For details regarding dates and venue for the next Flame Off, visit:

www.tuffnellglass.com
www.totallybeads.co.uk

Societies and Blog sites:

www.gbuk.org
www.frit-happens.co.uk
www.lampworketc.com
www.wetcanvas.com
www.cgs.org.uk
www.beadsociety.org.uk

Other:

www.friendsofbroadfieldhouse.co.uk
www.dudley.gov.uk/see-and-do/museums/glass-museum/
www.stourbridgebeadfair.co.uk
www.tempestglassbeadexhibition.org

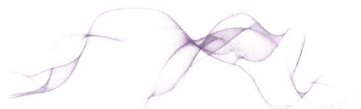

Some photos that did not fit into the main text of the book
but I thought they would be interesting and part of the History in the UK

GBUK AGM 2002

Intuitive ways to display your beads and jewellery!

Earring tree
Amanda Glanville 2003

Cake stand (non edible) Pauline Holt 2012

Kate Fowle Meleney

Loren Stump

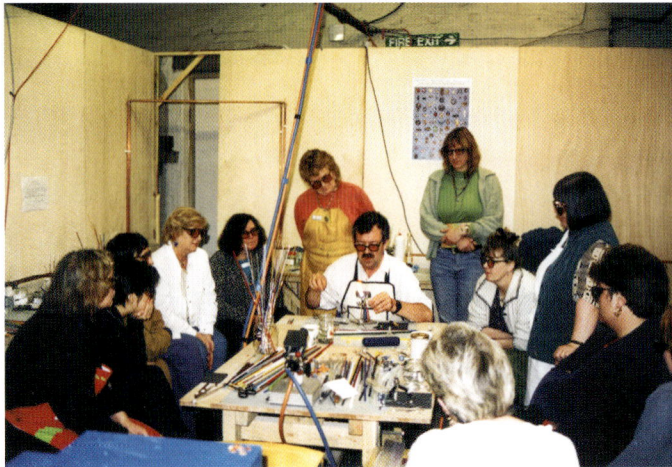

Group at 'Bring your Own Burner' week 1998

The Flame Off 2013

Ian Morle & Paddy Bush relaxing 2002

P&T Factory Tour

A selection of Lezlie Levitt-Wineberger's Beads

Di East at the Bonded Warehouse 2004

One of the displays at the International Festival of Glass 2004

Di East & Beverley Edwards at the GBUK AGM 2001

GBUK Promotional stand at the Harrow Bead Fair 2000
Another interesting display, note the clothes airer !